Religious Topics

THE HISTORY OF RELIGIONS

Jon Mayled

Religious Topics

Birth Customs
Death Customs
Family Life
Feasting and Fasting
Holy Books
Initiation Rites
Marriage Customs
Pilgrimage
Religious Art

Religious Beliefs
Religious Buildings
Religious Dress
Religious Festivals
Religious Food
Religious Services
Religious Symbols
Religious Teachers and Prophets
The History of Religions

Editor: Deborah Elliott

First published in 1987 by Wayland (Publishers) Limited
61 Western Road, Hove, East Sussex BN3 1JD, England

© Copyright 1987 Wayland (Publishers) Limited

British Library Cataloguing in Publication Data
Mayled, Jon
  The history of religion. – (Religious
  topics)
  1. Religions – Juvenile literature
  I. Title   II. Series
  291   BL92

  ISBN 1–85210–287–X

Phototypeset by Kalligraphics Ltd., Redhill, Surrey
Printed in Italy by G. Canale C.S.p.A., Turin
Bound in Belgium by Casterman S.A.

Cover: Guru Nanak, the founder of Sikhism, travelled widely spreading the word of God. Here he is shown with two followers on the back of a fish.

In this book, wherever we have used dates, we have used the abbreviations CE and BCE. These refer to the Common Era: after the year 1 when Jesus was born; and Before the Common Era.

Contents

Introduction

In any big city you will probably see the places of worship of many of the world's religions and also many of the people who belong to the major faiths.

Today, members of the world's religions are spread all over the world. In this book we shall try to discover where each religion began and how its members have come to be in so many parts of the world.

Muslims praying outside a mosque in Southall, London. Followers of Islam live all over the world.

You will see that Judaism, Christianity and Islam all come from the Middle East while Hinduism, Buddhism and Sikhism came from the Indian sub-continent. By looking at where and how these religions developed we shall be able to discover more about them and understand some of the differences and similarities between them.

Buddhist monks conduct a ceremony at the London Peace Pagoda.

Buddhism

Siddhartha Gautama, the Buddha, was born in 563 BCE in the village of Lumbini, in the Himalayan foothills. At the age of twenty-nine Siddhartha left his father's palace. For six years he travelled through northern India in an attempt to find an answer to the world's sufferings.

An ancient wall painting in China showing the Buddha travelling in a carriage.

A statue of the Golden Buddha in a temple in northern Thailand.

When Siddhartha reached the town of Bodh Gaya he sat down under a *bo* (fig) tree. He decided to stay there until he had solved the problem of the meaning of life. After forty-six days he finally reached the answer in the Four Noble Truths and the Eightfold Path.

For the next forty-five years, Siddhartha preached as a missionary. He gathered together a group of disciples who formed the *sangha*, the Buddhist order of monks.

A tenth-century Buddhist pagoda in Burma.

Siddhartha died in 483 BCE after eating some poisoned mushrooms. After his death the *sangha* continued but without a leader very little happened for the next two centuries. In the third century BCE, however, the Indian emperor, Asoka, became a Buddhist and spread the Buddha's teachings throughout India.

Asoka sent monks from India to spread the teachings of the Buddha south to Sri Lanka and as far east as Indonesia, Burma, Thailand, Cambodia (now called Kampuchea) and Laos. These southern Buddhists belong to the *Theravada* school. *Theravada* Buddhism stresses the importance of discipline and meditation.

During the first century BCE, northern or *Mahayana* Buddhism was established in China, Nepal and Tibet. It later spread to Vietnam, Korea and Japan. This school of Buddhism puts emphasis on devotion as well as meditation.

Two young Theravada Buddhist monks in Thailand.

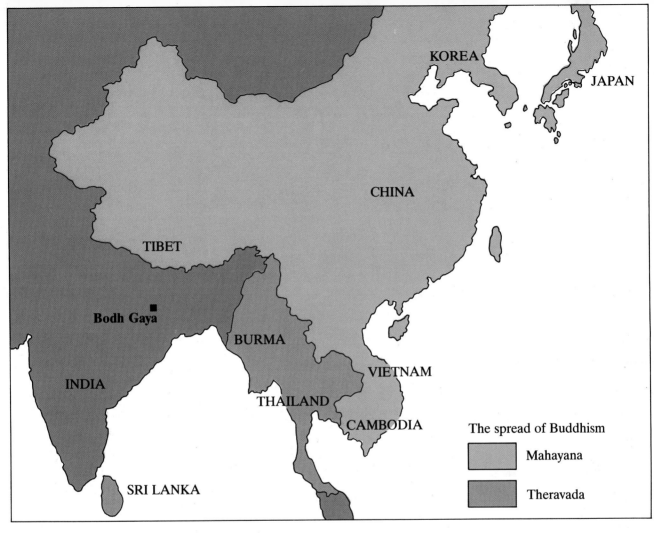

The spread of Buddhism

Mahayana

Theravada

Tibetan Buddhists believe that the noblest and most spiritual person should be their ruler. This person is called the Dalai Lama and is also the exiled ruler of Tibet.

The major areas of Mahayana *and* Theravada *Buddhism.*

10

Christianity

Jesus Christ, the son of God, was born in Bethlehem in Palestine. He spent most of his life with his parents in Nazareth. At this time the country was ruled by Romans.

From about the age of thirty, Jesus travelled around the countryside preaching. He soon attracted a large group of followers. After two or three years Jesus went to Jerusalem. There he was crucified (killed by being nailed to a cross) by the Romans because he claimed to be the King of Jews. The disciples continued to preach the message of Jesus.

Saint Paul was responsible for taking the teachings of Jesus out of Palestine. One day, on the road to Damascus, Paul had a vision of Jesus and decided to become a Christian. He made three long missionary journeys across the Mediterranean and was probably

Two Greek Orthodox Archbishops. In 1054 CE the Christian Church split into two groups: the Roman Catholic Church and the Orthodox Church.

executed in Rome in about 65 CE. The Roman Empire persecuted Jews for refusing to worship the Roman gods.

Christianity became a major religion when the Roman emperor, Constantine, allowed Christian worship in 313 CE. By 321 CE, Christianity was the official religion of the Roman Empire which extended all over Europe.

At first the only Church was the one which we now know as the Roman Catholic Church. In 1054 CE there was a final split between the Church based in Rome and the one which centred in Constantinople, now called Istanbul. There were a number of major disagreements between these two groups. They divided into two major bodies: the Roman Catholic Church whose head is the Pope in Rome and the Orthdox Church.

In the years leading up to the beginning of the seventeenth century CE, there were a number of people who protested against some of the teachings of the Roman Catholic

The Pope gives an audience to thousands of people in St. Peter's Square in the Vatican City, Rome. The Pope is head of the Roman Catholic Church.

Church. These included people such as Martin Luther and John Calvin. Eventually they set up a number of separate groups in the Christian Church who together are called Protestants. Protestants still believed in God and Jesus but worshipped them in a different way.

In the sixteenth century CE in England, King Henry VIII argued with the Pope over whether or not he could divorce his wife. The English church split away from the rule of the Pope and became established as the Church of England.

A young girl reads the lesson at a Church of England service. The Church of England became established in the sixteenth century CE, when King Henry VIII argued with the Pope over whether or not he could divorce his wife.

Hinduism

The Hindu religion began in the valley of the River Indus in Pakistan. More than 4,500 years ago, people lived in the Indus valley and built cities at Harappa and Mohenjo. They carved figures of dancers and animals on ivory and pottery seals. One of these seals,

A picture of Shiva *carved on to a seal, found in the Indus valley.*

Carvings in a Hindu temple in Patan, Nepal. Hinduism is believed to be one of the oldest religions in the world.

later discovered in the Indus valley, has a picture on it which some people think is the Hindu god, *Shiva*.

In about 1700 BCE a group of tribes, called Aryans, came from the north-west to live in this part of India. They were nomadic (travelling) people and worshipped their gods with a ceremonial fire. These two groups of people and their religions came together to form Hinduism.

A Hindu woman and her children in Jaipur, India. India is the major centre of Hinduism though Hindus live in many countries all over the world.

Although Buddhism had split away from Hinduism in the sixth century BCE, Hinduism remained the major religion of India. From the tenth century CE India was ruled by the Moghul emperors who were Muslims. Most people, however, remained Hindus.

Teachers and leaders such as Mahatma Gandhi have worked to change parts of the

Hindu religion. In particular they wished to change the way in which the lowest social group, the *pariahs*, were treated. Gandhi said they should be treated with great respect and called them *harijans* ('children of God').

This map shows the extent of the Hindu population in the Indian sub-continent.

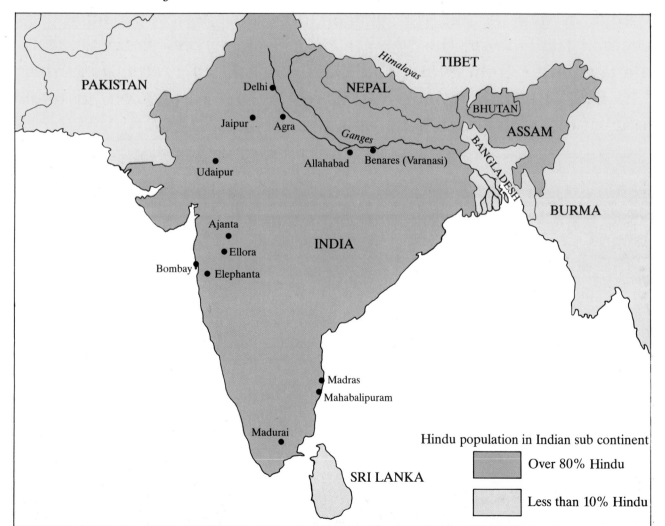

Islam

The Prophet Muhammad, the founder of Islam, was born in the city of Mecca in Saudi Arabia in 570 CE. At the age of forty he received the *Qur'an*, the Muslim holy book, in a revelation from *Allah* (God).

In 622 CE, Muhammad was asked by a group of his followers to help them in the city

The Prophet Muhammad is believed to have received the Qur'an *in a revelation from* Allah *(God), in about 610 CE.*

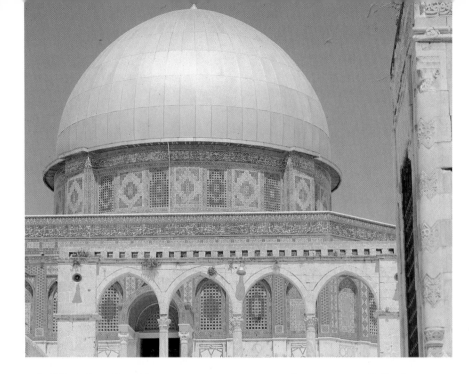

The Dome of the Rock was built on the site of Herod's Temple in Jerusalem.

of Yathrib. Despite many dangers Muhammad travelled to Yathrib and ruled the city. Here he built the first mosque of Islam. Later Yathrib was renamed Medinat-al-nabi (Medina) – 'the city of the Prophet'.

In 630 CE Egypt, Palestine, Syria, Iraq and the Persian Empire had all adopted the Muslim faith. In 690 CE the Mosque of Omar, or Dome of the Rock, was built on the site of Herod's Temple in Jerusalem.

A group of Muslims talking together outside a mosque. Islam is one of the most rapidly expanding religions.

In 711 CE Islam spread to Spain. Muslims remained there until the fifteenth century. By 1000 CE the message of Islam had been carried to China, India and across Central and West Africa.

After Muhammad's death his friend Abu Bakhr became his successor *(Khalifa)*. His cousin Ali, the fourth *Khalifa*, was murdered.

The supporters of Ali refused to accept the later *Khalifas* and instead followed Ali's relatives. These Muslims were known as *Shi'ites*. The modern ruler of Iran, the Ayatollah Khomeini, is a *Shi'ite* Muslim. The main centres of the *Shi'ite* movement are Iran, Yemen, Syria, Lebanon and Pakistan. Those Muslims

A Muslim father and son in London. Islam is one of the world's most popular religions. In Britain, about one thousand people a year adopt the Muslim faith. In the USA there are more than three million Muslims.

who continue to follow the *Khalifas* are the largest group, the *Sunni* Muslims.

The importance of the oil trade, based in the Middle East, brought Muslims to all parts of the world. Today, there are over 850 million Muslims in the world, including approximately 800,000 in Britain.

A map showing the distribution of Muslims.

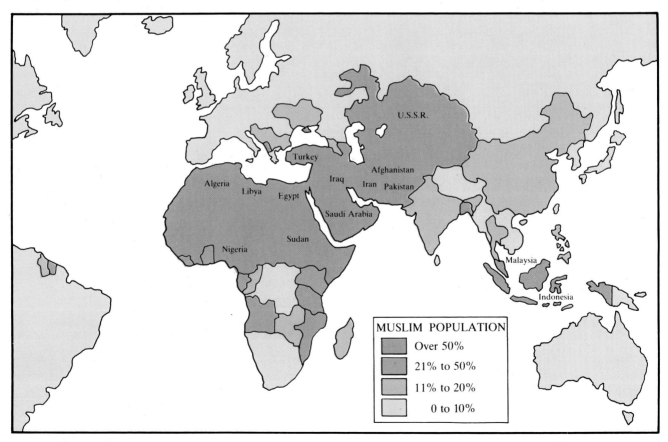

U.S.S.R.

Turkey

Afghanistan

Algeria

Iraq

Iran Pakistan

Libya

Egypt

Saudi Arabia

Sudan

Nigeria

Malaysia

Indonesia

MUSLIM POPULATION

Over 50%

21% to 50%

11% to 20%

0 to 10%

Judaism

Abraham, the founder of Judaism, was told by God to leave his home in Mesopotamia and move to Canaan. (Canaan was later called Israel and also Palestine.) God promised Abraham that he and his descendants would become a great nation in Canaan, if they worshipped God and obeyed

An illustration of Herod's Temple in Jerusalem. The Temple was the centre of worship for the Jews because the Ten Commandments, given to them by God, were stored there.

Visitors at the Western Wall, the last remaining wall of Herod's Temple in Jerusalem.

His laws. This is why Jews believe they have been chosen to make God known to the world. Many years later, because of famine, they had to move to Egypt. There the Jews were forced to become slaves of the Pharaoh. The Biblical story of the Exodus charts their forty year journey, led by Moses, back to Canaan in about 1250 BCE.

After this the Jews were conquered by the Philistines. In 605 BCE they became the subjects of the Babylonians under King Nebuchadnezzar. In 586 BCE the Jews were taken to Babylon while Jerusalem and the Temple were destroyed. In 538 BCE the Babylonians were conquered by the Persians. The Jews were sent back to Jerusalem and the Temple was rebuilt.

The expansion of first the Greek and then the Roman Empire reached Israel and in 63 BCE it became a Roman province. The Temple was again destroyed in 70 CE.

Later, Jerusalem became a Muslim city

and many Jews moved elsewhere. Jewish communities were established in Spain and Portugal and all over Eastern Europe. This body of Jews outside of Israel is said to be living in the 'Diaspora'. From the fifteenth to the eighteenth century CE, all over Europe, Jews were persecuted for their beliefs. Many Jews were put to death by the Spanish Inquisition for refusing to become Christians.

A Jewish family leaving a synagogue in London. The present Jewish community in Britain goes back to 1656 CE and numbers approximately 333,000.

Gradually Jews were given the same rights as everyone else. Between 1935 and 1945 CE more than six million Jews were put to death by the Nazi government of Germany, in the terrible 'holocaust'.

In 1948 CE the Jews were finally granted their wish to return to the Promised Land when the Jewish State of Israel was established in what had previously been Palestine.

A street in modern day Jerusalem. The world population of Jews is estimated at 15 million. Only 23 per cent live in Israel. Nearly twice as many Jews live in the USA as in Israel.

Sikhism

Guru Nanak, the founder of Sikhism, was born in the village of Talwandi (now called Nanakana) in modern Pakistan. Sikhs believe that, after a revelation (message)

Guru Nanak. Sikhism is one of the youngest of the world's major religions. It was founded by Guru Nanak in 1469 CE in a part of northern India called the Punjab.

*A Sikh temple
ceremony in Kenya.
After their homeland
was divided up in
1947 CE, many Sikhs
went to live in Africa.*

from God, Guru Nanak travelled for thirty years on a missionary journey. He is believed to have visited the Muslim holy city of Mecca in Saudi Arabia and travelled back through Bengal.

In 1521 CE Guru Nanak stopped travelling and set up a new town in the Punjab, which he called Kartarpur. There he established a Sikh community.

During the eighteenth century CE the Muslim Empire moved into north-west India. By 1799 CE, however, the Sikhs had reclaimed the Punjab as an independent state.

Almost 500,000 Sikhs died trying to prevent their homeland of the Punjab being divided up between Pakistan and India in 1947 CE. The Sikh holy city of Amritsar is still in India. Many Sikhs were driven out of Pakistan and went to live in East Africa and Britain. Some of these were again forced to leave the African State of Uganda in 1972 CE by the President.

In 1966 CE the Indian government recognized the Punjab as being a Sikh province. Today there are about fifteen million Sikhs and over half a million of these live in Britain.

Sikhism has spread from India to Britain, the USA and Australia.

Glossary

Disciples The name given to Jesus's twelve original companions, and to anyone who follows him now.

Holocaust The murder of six million Jews by Nazi Germany between 1935 and 1945 CE.

Independent Free from control by others.

Meditation To think very deeply about something.

Missionary A person who travels around spreading a particular religious belief.

Nomadic A way of life whereby a group of people, without a fixed home, wander from place to place.

Pharaoh The title given to the ancient Egyptian kings.

Pope The leader of the Roman Catholic Church who lives in the Vatican, a district in Rome.

Spanish Inquisition An institution from the fifteenth to the seventeenth century which wanted to keep Spain Catholic and so persecuted non-Catholics.

Further Reading

If you would like to find out more about the history of religions you may like to read the following books:

Beliefs and Believers series – published by Wayland

Believers All – published by Blackie

Exploring Religion series – published by Bell and Hyman

Worship series – published by Holt Saunders

Religions of Man – published by Stanley Thornes

Religions of the World series – published by Wayland

The following videos are very helpful:

Looking at Faith – produced by CEM Video.

Through the Eyes series – produced by CEM Video.

Acknowledgements

The publisher would like to thank the following for providing the pictures for the book: Bruce Coleman Ltd 15; Hutchison Library 4, 6, 9, 21, 25, 28, 29; Ann and Bury Peerlees 11, 13, 14, 27; Sri Lankan Tourist Board 5; Topham 23; Malcolm S. Walker 10, 17, 22; Wayland Picture Library 18, 22; Zefa 7, 8, 12, 16, 19, 20, 24, 26.

Index